Profiles in Greek and Roman Mythology

HERMES

Mitchell Lane
PUBLISHERS

P.O. Box 196
Hockessin, Delaware 19707
Visit us on the web: www.mitchelllane.com
Comments? email us: mitchelllane@mitchelllane.com

PROFILES IN GREEK AND ROMAN MYTHOLOGY

Titles in the Series

Profiles in Greek and Roman Mythology

HERMES

Kayleen Reusser

Mitchell Lane

PUBLISHERS

P.O. Box 196
Hockessin, Delaware 19707
Visit us on the web: www.mitchelllane.com
Comments? email us: mitchelllane@mitchelllane.com

PUBLISHERS

Printing   1   2   3   4   5   6   7   8   9

Library of Congress Cataloging-in-Publication Data
Reusser, Kayleen.
  Hermes / by Kayleen Reusser.
      p. cm. — (Profiles in Greek and Roman mythology)
  Includes bibliographical references (p.   ) and index.
  ISBN 978-1-58415-748-9 (library bound)
  1. Hermes (Greek deity)—Juvenile literature. I. Title.
  BL820.M5R48 2010
  398.20938'01—dc22

                                                                    2009045664

ABOUT THE AUTHOR: Kayleen Reusser has written several children's books, including biographies on Selena Gomez, Leona Lewis, and Taylor Swift. She is also the author of *Hephaestus* and *Hades* in this series. She lives in the Midwest with her family. Find out more about Kayleen at www.KayleenR.com.

AUTHOR'S NOTE: The stories retold in this book use dialog as an aid to readability. The dialog is based on the author's research.

PUBLISHER'S NOTE: This story is based on the author's extensive research, which she believes to be accurate. Documentation of such research is contained on page 46.

The internet sites referenced herein were active as of the publication date. Due to the fleeting nature of some web sites, we cannot guarantee they will all be active when you are reading this book.

To reflect current usage, we have chosen to use the secular era designations BCE ("before the common era") and CE ("of the common era") instead of the traditional designations BC ("before Christ") and AD (*anno Domini*, "in the year of the Lord").

TABLE OF CONTENTS

Profiles in Greek and Roman Mythology

A statue of Hermes, the messenger god, stands in Rome's famous Palazzo Altemps. This reproduction from the first or second century CE is a copy of a Greek original, carved in the fifth century BCE. When the Romans adopted the Greek gods into their pantheon, they called the messenger god Mercury.

CHAPTER 1

A Miraculous Birth

Ping! Pang! Pung!

Hermes (HUR-meez) plucked the strings of his lyre and smiled, pleased with the instrument's melodic sound. He spent several minutes composing a lively tune. As he added humorous words to accompany the ditty, birds and small animals of the forest stopped to listen.

Suddenly, Hermes stopped playing. Bending his ear to the mouth of a nearby cave, he held his breath. Had his mother awakened from her nap? She and her nurse Cyllene (sih-LEEN) would scold him for getting out of his cradle.

Hermes had been born that morning to the nymph Maia (MY-uh). His father was Zeus (ZOOS), king of the gods. This made Hermes a god. As was the case with most gods, Hermes grew fast, so that by noon of his first day, he could walk and run. After waking from his first nap, he had climbed from his cradle and toddled to the entrance of the cave.

When Hermes had looked out at the vast world, the first thing he saw was a tortoise. He had never seen that or any animal and was fascinated by what he thought was a toy. He took the tortoise, removed its shell, and fastened some stringy sheep innards across the inside. As he slid his tiny fingers up and down the strings, he nimbly played a beautiful melody on his musical invention.[1]

Still listening at the cave's entrance, Hermes heard nothing but Maia's deep, relaxed breathing issuing from inside. He breathed a sigh of relief. His mother and Cyllene would sleep until late in the afternoon. Tiring of the lyre, Hermes tossed it aside and walked

away, determined to have an adventure before his mother and Cyl-lene awoke.

He walked down a road for several hours, his eyes wide with curiosity. When he saw a herd of cows in a pasture, Hermes, full of mischief, had an idea. Hiding in the grasses around the pasture, he separated fifty of the best cows, thinking to lead them to his cave.

Fearing someone would follow the herd, Hermes made shoes for himself and the cows from oak bark, attaching them with plaited grass. He then forced the cattle to follow him this way and that over the sandy ground. He even had them walk backward, hoping to con-fuse those who might follow their trail.

An old man, watching his own herd, scratched his head as he watched Hermes chase the cattle in a zigzag pattern. He called out, "What are you doing, child?"

Hermes' mind raced to come up with an excuse. "I'm taking a gift of these cows to my lovely mother," he said. "She will enjoy see-ing them and the shoes I've made for them. It's a secret, so please don't tell anyone." He looked up at the man with a big grin on his round face, opened his eyes wide, and giggled behind fingers held over his mouth.

Hermes seemed so small and innocent that the man nodded, though he continued to watch the strange-looking group parade down the road.

Before he got home, Hermes sacrificed two of the cows to the Olympic gods. Thinking his mother would like the hides of the slain cows for blankets, he carried them while leading the rest of the cows into the woods behind the cave where his mother slept.

The march took most of the night. Just as the rosy streaks of dawn dotted the horizon, Hermes, who was just one day old, tied his new herd to the trees behind the cave. Then he hung up the hides to dry, slipped into his cradle, pulled his blankets to his chin, and fell asleep.

One of the most popular myths about Hermes includes his theft of Apollo's cows. The Greeks preserved the story in pottery.

A few hours later, the Greek god Apollo (uh-PAH-loh) entered the pasture where he had left his herd to graze. The sun shone brightly, and the birds sang a happy tune, but Apollo's mind filled with dread as he stood in the middle of the empty field. No contented sounds of munching could be heard. His heart sank as he walked the breadth of the field. With each step, he grew more incredulous.

His herd had disappeared! Who could have taken them?

In the soft grass, Apollo studied the tracks that went every way. Then he spied tiny footprints. Could the thief have been a child?

Apollo set out to find his cows. He traveled from land to land, looking for clues of his herd's whereabouts. He even offered a reward for information about the theft, but no one knew anything.

One day an old man approached Apollo. "I may have been dreaming," he said, "but a while ago I saw an infant herd some cattle down this road. It was a funny sight. He drove them backward."

"Where did the child take the herd?" Apollo demanded.

The man pointed toward the mountains of Arcadia (ar-KAY-dee-uh). Apollo knew of no baby born there, but he thanked the man, paid him the reward, and set off in search of the mysterious child.

As Apollo passed through Arcadia, he met the nymph Cyllene, gathering water at a stream. "The most wonderful thing has happened," she babbled. "A gifted child of Zeus was born recently to the nymph Maia. He is the best baby in Arcadia, and I'm his nurse." She showed Apollo the lyre Hermes had made from a tortoiseshell. "He created this while his mother and I slept. He is a genius!"[2]

Apollo accepted the nurse's offer to meet the wondrous babe and accompanied her inside the cave.

Hermes had awakened by the time they arrived. When he heard Apollo greet Maia, he stuck his thumb in his mouth, closed his eyes, and pretended to be asleep. He didn't know Apollo but was suspicious of strangers.

Hermes had good reason to be afraid. As Apollo peered at Hermes in his crib, supposedly enthralled with the wondrous babe, his ire grew. With fine baby hair curled into a question mark and a soft, plump body, Hermes looked like any slumbering infant. But Apollo had seen the two hides from his herd hanging on a hook in the cave and knew he had his thief. Gritting his teeth in frustration, he began yanking open cupboards and pulling aside furniture.[3]

"What are you doing?" Maia shouted.

"I'm looking for my cows," he said. "I think your baby has taken them."

Maia stared at him, mouth agape. Cyllene stopped stirring Maia's porridge, equally shocked. Apollo leaned over Hermes' bed, his hands gripping the rails. "Where are my cows?" he shouted. "I

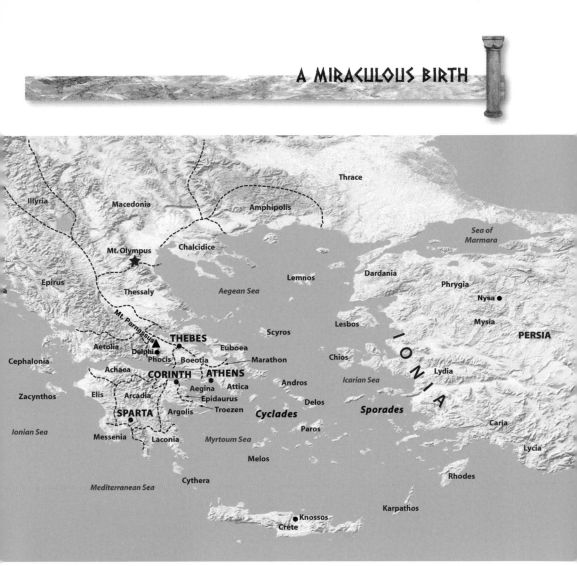

Ancient Greece was made up of dozens of city-states. Hermes was born in the mountains of Arcadia.

Hermes was the son of Zeus, king of the gods, and Maia, one of the Pleiades. The Pleiades, or Seven Sisters, were immortalized in the constellation of the same name.

demand you tell me or you'll be stealing from the children of Tartarus [TAR-ter-us]."

"Are you accusing this poor child of being a thief?" asked Cyllene, surprise lifting her eyebrows to her hairline. "That's ridiculous!"

Maia pointed to her baby, still wrapped in baby clothes. "Hermes is a mere baby. He could not be a thief!"

Hermes sat up in his cradle. "You're not thinking clearly," he told Apollo calmly. "I was born yesterday. How could I guide a herd of cows? All I know are diapers, blankets, and sleep."

Apollo picked up the baby. "Since you won't take me to my cows, I will take you to our father," he said sternly. "Zeus will judge if you are a thief." Then he carried Hermes, crying in protest, from the cave to Mount Olympus (oh-LIM-pus).[4]

Hermes may have started out small, but from his birth he had a mighty impact on everyone around him. Nestled in his cradle, looking up at the face of the powerful Apollo, little Hermes had no fear and plenty of wit. As he grew older, he became more adept at talking his way out of tricky situations. Hermes' skill in communication would earn him the title of god of learning, memory, poetry, and business. His equivalent among the Roman gods was Mercury. From his name we get the word merchandise. Of course, he was also known as the god of thievery![5]

Of all gods, Hermes was the shrewdest and most cunning. Ironically, he appears more often in tales of mythology than any other god.[6]

Hermes coin

front   back

Just as we in the twenty-first century love to watch movies that involve a chase, it seems the Greeks were also enthralled by this god's devious exploits. But Hermes was not all bad, as Apollo was soon to learn.

Hermes Saves His Father

for your info

F.Y.I.

According to Greek myth, a place in the Underworld, Tartarus, collaborated with Gaea (GY-uh), the earth, to create a family of monsters. Typhon (TY-fon), a fire-breathing, hurricane-spawning giant, was the most dangerous.

Vase painting of Typhon

Typhon was the largest monster ever born. From his thighs down he was nothing but coiled serpents. His arms when he spread them out reached 100 leagues in both directions. Instead of hands, he had countless serpents' heads. His head, shaped like a donkey's, touched the stars. His wings darkened the sun. Fire flashed from his eyes, and flaming rocks hurtled from his mouth.

One day, Typhon rushed toward Olympus, and the gods, including Zeus, fled in terror. Only Athena (uh-THEE-nuh), the goddess of war, stood her ground, taunting Zeus for his cowardice. The king of the gods returned, sending many of his deadly thunderbolts at Typhon. A slash of his sickle wounded Typhon, and the great monster retreated to Mount Cassius (KASH-us), which looms on the border of Turkey and Syria.

Soon Zeus caught up with Typhon and the two grappled in a duel. Typhon twined his myriad coils about Zeus, disarming him by severing the sinews of his hands and feet. He dragged Zeus into a cave and hid the sinews in a fur rug under a serpent-monster.

Zeus could not move. He might have lain there forever and Olympus would have lost its mighty king if Hermes had not discovered the location of the sinews. Upon grabbing the prized pieces, Hermes rushed them to Zeus' side, replacing them on the king's limbs.

Zeus returned to Mount Olympus, where he snatched a cache of thunderbolts with which to fight Typhon. Racing toward it in a chariot, he fought the deadly monster. After a prolonged contest, Zeus trapped Typhon under Mount Etna, where it is said the fiercest child of Tartarus still breathes fire today.[7]

A detail from Sandro Botticelli's 1482 painting *La Primavera* (Spring) shows Hermes using his staff to protect the Three Graces (Grace, Beauty, and Joy) from wintry winds.

Apollo carried Hermes and the cow hides to Mount Olympus, where Zeus held council with other gods and goddesses. Zeus listened to Apollo's tale of complaint, then turned to Hermes. "Who are you, little boy?" he asked.

Hermes stood tall. "Father, I am your son, Hermes. I was born yesterday to the nymph Maia."

Zeus smiled and patted Hermes on the head. "Then you must certainly be innocent of this crime."

"Of course I am, father!" cried Hermes. "I don't know what this god is talking about. He came to the cave where my mother and I live, looking for his cows. Do I look like a thief who could have steered cows down a road?" To reinforce his argument, he held a soft blanket next to his face and opened his eyes wide to give a look of innocence.

Apollo was not fooled. His voice shook with anger as he pointed a finger at Hermes. "He stole my cows! He must return them!"

Apollo had expected Zeus to command Hermes to return the cows after hearing the story. Instead, Zeus seemed annoyed that he had been disturbed. "How do you think a babe like this could have made cows walk backward and then hide them?" he asked Apollo.

"I have an eyewitness who says a child led the cows in the direction of Arcadia," Apollo said.

"Who is this witness?"

Apollo explained the old man's story. Zeus looked hard at his youngest son. "Hermes, you offer a first-class explanation, but now I fear your deeds have been brought to light. You must return your brother's cows to him."

Hermes hung his head. "You are right, Father. Yesterday I was too young to know right from wrong. I admit I stole the cows that belonged to Apollo and beg your pardon." Then he turned to Apollo. "I am sorry to have taken your cows and I pledge against the River Styx never to steal from you again. You may have them back, except for the two I cut up into twelve equal portions as a sacrifice to the twelve gods."

"There are only eleven gods," said Apollo, and he counted them off: "Zeus, Hera [HAYR-uh], Poseidon [poh-SY-dun], Hestia [HES-tee-uh], Demeter [DIH-meh-ter], Artemis [AR-tuh-mis], Ares [AYR-eez], Athena, Hephaestus [heh-FES-tus], Aphrodite [af-roh-DY-tee], and I. Who is the twelfth?"

Hermes bowed. "Yours truly."

Apollo laughed. He couldn't help it. Hermes was only a baby, but he had a healthy self-esteem. "Let us go retrieve my cows, brother. I am no longer angry at you and wish to be your friend."

Hermes led Apollo behind the cave where he had hidden the cows. Before Apollo left, Hermes took out his lyre and began to play and sing. Apollo was delighted with the rapturous tunes that floated on the breeze.

"What is that instrument?" asked Apollo, closing his eyes in relaxation.

"It is a lyre made from a tortoiseshell," Hermes said. He strummed a tune praising Apollo's nobility, intelligence, and generosity.

"Play more on your stringed instrument," Apollo told the child. "It pleases my soul to hear you sing."

After Hermes had sung several more tunes, Apollo said, "I insist you trade me your lyre for my cows. I would rather hear beautiful music than care for smelly cattle."

Hermes handed him the handmade lyre. "My gift to you, brother," he said. "Play well."

The resourceful Hermes cut some plants into reeds, shaping them into a shepherd's pipe. As he played another tune on his newest

instrument, Apollo demanded it as well. "If you give me that pipe, Hermes, I will give you this golden staff, which I use to herd my cattle. In the future, you shall be god of herdsmen and shepherds."

"My pipe is worth more than your staff," said Hermes. "But I will make the exchange if you teach me how to tell the future. That seems to be a useful art."

Apollo protested. "I can't do that, but if you go to my old nurse who lives on Parnassus [par-NAS-us], a mountain in Phocis, she will teach you how to tell the future from pebbles."

Hermes agreed and they shook hands. Both gods returned to Olympus to tell Zeus the affair had been settled.[1]

Upon first meeting the infant Hermes, Apollo mistrusts him, but soon forgets his doubts. Hermes gives Apollo his lyre, and Apollo gives Hermes his staff.

After listening to the story, Zeus smiled in satisfaction. He put Hermes on his knee. "Now, my son, you seem to be a smart and persuasive godling. Take care in the future not to steal or tell lies. You are a good boy and must respect the rights and property of others."

"I will obey you, Father," said Hermes, "though I can't promise always to tell the truth."

"You are still a child and that would not be expected of you," said Zeus, with a smile.

Hermes turned as if to go to Maia's grotto, then faced Zeus. "I have a request, Father."

"What is it, my child?"

"I ask that you make me your messenger," Hermes replied. "I will carry your important messages throughout your kingdom and be responsible for the safety of all of your property."

Zeus rubbed his chin. "I have never had a personal messenger, but there is often a need for one." He stood, thinking, then said, "I will give you the responsibilities you have asked for, Hermes, and the duties of making treaties, the promotion of business, and the safety of travelers on any road in the world."

Hermes' gift of always knowing the right words to say were just what Zeus needed. As an attaché, Hermes was responsible for conveying the king's desires and commands. This could prove challenging when the one receiving the news did not agree with the king's edict. In those instances the king had to rely on his messenger to stand firm and not compromise. If a king's word was not considered law, chaos would rule the land.

Zeus handed Hermes a herald's staff with white ribbons. "Everyone in the world is to respect this staff and its bearer," he announced. He also gave Hermes a round hat to shield his face against the rain, and winged golden sandals. "These items will carry you about with the swiftness of the wind."[2]

With the staff and sandals, Hermes was welcome everywhere. He worked hard to make himself useful to those he met. He taught

In art, Hermes is often shown wearing winged shoes and hat while carrying a caduceus—a herald's (or messenger's) staff with two intertwined serpents. The staff, with its two snakes, came to symbolize peace. It has often been confused with the staff of Asklepios, which symbolizes medicine and has only one snake.

the Olympic family of gods and goddesses the art of making a fire by rapidly twirling a fire stick. He became the god of arithmetic, astronomy, musical scales, weights and measures, boxing, and gymnastics.[3]

Other gods recognized Hermes' good qualities and asked him for assistance. Hades appointed him as the conductor of the dead to the Underworld. "Lay your golden staff on the eyes of the dying and lead them gently to the realm of the dead," he instructed Hermes.[4] No other god was allowed to travel between Mount Olympus and Hades. Once a soul entered the Underworld, it could never leave.

Artemis, the goddess of war, took Hermes hunting with her.

Still, Hermes' life was not easy. Zeus often assigned him jobs that no one else was swift or brave enough to accomplish. Some of his most harrowing assignments were to outsmart ferocious monsters. It would take every bit of his cunning and courage to win the battles set before him.

Hermes may have looked innocent as he held a shepherd's pipe, but the god of thieves had a tricky side that often confounded others.

The Greek Alphabet

Scholars believe the first written alphabet was developed in Egypt around 1800 BCE. Travelers and traders to Greece carried it across the sea, where the Greeks became the first Europeans to write with an alphabet. After the collapse of Greek civilization around 1200 BCE, writing disappeared from Greece.

Hundreds of years passed, and Greek civilization flourished again. With the conquests of Alexander the Great (336–323 BCE), the Greek language and alphabet entered the Near East, where it underwent changes. Eventually, the people who lived there adopted it as their second language.

When Greece won its freedom from the Turks in 1830, Athens became the capital of a unified Greece. Changes again occurred to the Greek alphabet, but eventually the language spoken and written in Athens became the basis for communication everywhere in the country.[5]

In Greek mythology, Hermes is credited for inventing the Greek alphabet. He presumably carried the alphabet system from Egypt to Greece, as the Greek alphabet was a simplified version of Egyptian hieroglyphs (HY-roh-glifs).[6] The first letter he wrote was in the shape of a V. He held the crane sacred, and cranes fly in a V formation.[7]

The Three Fates—goddesses who determined a person's future—may have assisted Hermes in composing the alphabet. They invented the vowels—alpha (A), iota (I), omicron (O), and upsilon (Y)—and consonants beta (B) and tau (T). The Fates' alphabet was closely linked with the calendar. Its letters were represented not by written characters but by twigs cut from different trees.[8]

A	**B**	**Γ**	**Δ**	**E**	**Z**
Alpha (al-fah)	Beta (bay-tah)	Gamma (gam-ah)	Delta (del-ta)	Epsilon (ep-si-lon)	Zeta (zay-tah)
H	**Θ**	**I**	**K**	**Λ**	**M**
Eta (ay-tah)	Theta (thay-tah)	Iota (eye-o-tah)	Kappa (cap-pah)	Lambda (lamb-dah)	Mu (mew)
N	**Ξ**	**O**	**Π**	**P**	**Σ**
Nu (new)	Xi (zie)	Omicron (om-e-cron)	Pi (pie)	Rho (roe)	Sigma (sig-mah)
T	**Y**	**Φ**	**X**	**Ψ**	**Ω**
Tau (taw)	Upsilon (up-si-lon)	Phi (fie)	Chi (kie)	Psi (sigh)	Omega (oh-may-gah)

Greek alphabet

In this painting by Bartholomaeus Spranger (1585), Hermes and the goddess Athena aid Perseus with weapons to overcome the monster Medusa.

HERMES

⟨HAPTER 3

Hermes the Spy and Guide

As Zeus' herald, Hermes often delivered important messages to gods and goddesses. Sometimes Zeus sent Hermes out not to deliver, but to gather important information. In other words, Hermes was a spy.

Zeus had fallen in love with the nymph Io (EYE-oh). Zeus' wife, Hera, was jealous of Zeus' girlfriends (he had several), so when Zeus visited Io on the island of Argos, he covered the two of them with a thick, dark cloud.

One day, Hera noticed that Zeus was missing from his throne. She looked for him in many lands but could find no trace of him. Finally, upon seeing a dark cloud over the island of Argos, she thought, "That's strange. The rest of the sky is blue."

Hera flew to the island, waving her arms to disperse the cloud. Zeus, hiding inside the cloud with Io, quickly disguised Io as a white heifer.

When the cloud dissipated, Hera saw her husband holding the horn of a young cow. "What do you have, my lord?" she asked suspiciously.

"A simple cow," Zeus replied, smiling. "I found her wandering on the hillside and thought she would make a wonderful gift for you."

Hera sniffed. "I thought you were with the nymph Io, whom you love so much."

Zeus smiled. "My dear wife, it is you I love," he said. He started to lead the animal away. "To prove my love, I'll have her delivered to you immediately." He secretly planned to "lose" the cow along the way.

"Never mind, I'll take her myself," snapped Hera, not trusting Zeus' story or his declaration of devotion. Grabbing the heifer's horn from Zeus, she strode angrily away. Io, trapped inside the body of the cow, mooed mournfully at Zeus, who gazed after her with longing.

The queen of the gods led the cow over several hills. Finally, they stopped beside a sturdy olive tree. Hera tied the beast to the tree, then appointed her favorite monster, Argos, to stand guard. "Keep this cow tethered to the tree," she said. "Don't take your eyes off her."

Hera had picked a good guard, for Argos had 100 eyes. When some eyes slept, others stayed open. If someone tried to untie Io, Argos would stop the intruder by bashing him over the head. Io would never escape.

Zeus missed his beloved Io. From his throne on Mount Olympus, he could hear her mooing in misery.

Zeus sent for Hermes. "Son, you must trick Argos into closing all of his eyes," he said. "Then you can rescue Io."

Hermes knew Argos never slept. How could he steal Io without the monster knowing about it? After thinking about it for days, an idea finally came to him.

Speeding down to earth, he hid the cap and wings that marked him as a god. Keeping only a staff, he disguised himself as a wandering shepherd, and coaxed a flock of wild goats to follow him to a meadow near Io and Argos. He pulled out his shepherd's pipe and began to play a melodic song, much as he had played for Apollo on his lyre.

Like Apollo, Argos was enchanted by the music. Without being aware of it, some of his eyes shut in relaxation. He called out to Hermes, "Shepherd, I wish to hear more of your music. Come closer."

Hermes plopped down next to the monster with a friendly smile, no hint of mischief in his demeanor. All day he sang and talked to

German artist Peter Paul Rubens shows Hermes rescuing Io, who has been transformed into a cow. In the painting, the sleeping Argos appears to have only two eyes.

Argos about the lives of the gods and goddesses who lived on Olympus. The stories at times confused Argos, but the monster enjoyed the company of his new soft-spoken friend. Soon, though he fought to keep some of his eyes open, more of them fell shut.

As the hours passed, Hermes never turned his gaze from Argos, nor did he raise his voice in frustration. Patiently, he watched as dozens of the monster's eyelids slid closed. By the time the sun passed over the horizon, Argos had lost the battle and the last of his eyes closed in peaceful slumber. Hermes quickly hit Argos over the head, then cut Io free from her halter. "Flee!" he cried.

The little heifer galloped happily away. Hastily donning his special messenger's cap and sandals, Hermes returned to Olympus.

When Hera saw what had happened to Argos, she grieved for her fallen friend. Then she took all of Argos' eyes and put them in the tail feathers of the peacock, where they can be seen to this day.[1]

Because he killed Argos, Hermes was called Argeiphontes, "slayer of Argos."[2]

Another story involving Hermes, Zeus, and a jealous Hera concerns the birth of Dionysus (dy-oh-NY-sus). Semele (SEH-muh-lee), a mortal woman, was to have a child by Zeus. The jealous Hera had Semele killed, but Zeus rescued the baby. He sewed him into the skin of his thigh until it was time for the baby to be born. Still wary of Hera's rage, Zeus looked for ways to keep Dionysus hidden from his wife. He asked Hermes to find a safe place for the boy to be raised. After the birth, Hermes took him to the Maenads (MAY-nadz), nymphs who lived in the valley of Nysa. Dionysus became the immortal god of wine, taking the place of Hestia as one of the twelve Olympians.

Besides bearing messages and running other errands for Zeus, Hermes acted as a guide. Because he led the souls of the dead—and sometimes the living—to Hades and back,[3] he was sometimes called Psychopompos, "conductor of souls."

As a guide for Athena, Hera, and Aphrodite to Mount Ida, he had a hand in fomenting the Trojan War. Eris, or Strife, had thrown a golden apple, inscribed with the words "for the fairest," into a gathering of the gods. Athena, Hera, and Aphrodite fought over the apple, each believing that she was the fairest. Hermes took them to Mount Ida, where Paris, a prince of Troy, would judge their beauty.[4] The goddesses each offered Paris a gift if he should choose her, and Paris chose Aphrodite, who promised him the most beautiful woman in the world. That woman was Helen, the wife of the king of Sparta, and her abduction to Troy by Paris sparked the ten-year Trojan War.

Near the end of the war, as told in Book 24 of *The Iliad*, Hermes guided King Priam through the enemy camp to Achilles' tent. There

Priam requested that Achilles, who had slain Priam's son Hector, release Hector's body so that Priam could give him an honorable funeral. After recalling his own feelings for his slain father, Achilles agreed to do so.[5]

In one instance, Hermes' ability to deliver important messages for Zeus affected the destiny of the world.

The god of the Underworld, Hades, had kidnapped Persephone (per-SEH-fuh-nee), whom he wanted to serve as his queen. Persephone's mother, Demeter, ached for her missing daughter. Since Demeter was the goddess of growing things, nothing grew on earth because she was consumed with grief. People began to starve.

When Zeus saw mortals had no rain and no food, he sent other gods to Demeter to convince her to send rain. She would not listen. "Nothing on earth will bear fruit until my daughter returns to me!" she cried.

Zeus knew he must send someone to Hades to convince the king of the Underworld to give up his bride. He called for Hermes. "Tell Hades that Zeus commands him to allow Persephone to return to her mother. Demeter has neglected the care of the earth and the people are hungry."

As Hermes flew off to do Zeus' bidding, Zeus said to Demeter, "If Persephone has not yet eaten the food of the dead, she may return to Olympus. But if she has eaten in Hades, she must remain there." Certain her daughter would rather starve than eat Hades' food, Demeter held her breath in anticipation of seeing Persephone again.

After crossing the murky River Styx and flying past the three-headed dog that guarded the gates to the Underworld, Hermes found Hades and his bride sitting on their thrones. Persephone's skin was a sickly gray. Hades appeared exuberant.

"My lord, your brother and the great king of the gods, Zeus, greets you and wishes you well," Hermes announced.

Hades bowed his head, acknowledging his brother's mighty rule over heaven and earth. "What brings the messenger god to the Abode of the Dead?"

"Your brother requests you release Persephone so that she may return to her mother," Hermes said. "Demeter misses her daughter and in her grief has forgotten her duties as mother of the harvest."

At first Hades seemed not to hear Hermes' request. Hours of pleading by both Hermes and Persephone finally convinced him to yield. "Persephone may leave if she has not eaten any food while living in the Underworld," said Hades.

Persephone's eyes sparkled. "I have not eaten even a crumb of bread during my stay," she said.

"Have you forgotten, my dear, this morning when I fed you a pomegranate seed from my underground orchard? You found it quite delicious."

Persephone shrank back in despair.

Hermes intervened. "Perhaps an agreement can be reached," he said.

Since Persephone had eaten in the Underworld, Demeter agreed that Persephone had to live in Hades six months of the year. The rest of the time, Persephone spent with her mother on Earth. The Greeks believed that the time Persephone spent in Hades were the months of winter. The months she spent with Demeter were spring and summer.[6]

Hermes may have only been the king's messenger, but his ability to handle, and often diffuse, a tense situation reflected Zeus' judgment. In this story, conditions on Earth were stark because of Demeter's grief. If Demeter continued to forget her responsibilities, she would have brought an end to civilization. In the negotiations, Hades' role as a god and as Zeus' brother had to be considered. Hermes' ability to convince both sides to compromise demonstrated that a peaceful resolution could be reached between the gods.

Perseus and Medusa

Perseus had a difficult assignment: he needed to kill the monster Medusa. King Polydectes had kidnapped Perseus' mother, Danae, and promised to release her if Perseus could bring him the head of Medusa.

The job was not easy. Medusa had once been beautiful, but a jealous goddess had changed her into a monster. Her head was covered with vicious snakes, and anyone who looked her in the eye turned to stone. She lived in a cave with her Gorgon sisters.

Hermes and Athena came to Perseus' aid. They instructed him to visit sisters of the Gorgons, the Graeae, who had only one eye and one tooth between them. Perseus tricked them, and convinced them to help him with his mission. They told him where to find a particular group of nymphs. These nymphs loaned him winged sandals, which could help him fly to Medusa and escape; a cap of invisibility from Hades; and a magic wallet that could hold Medusa's head. He also carried Athena's shield, which had a mirror-like finish, and a sword from Hermes.

Perseus flew to Medusa's cave. Wearing the cap of invisibility and bearing the shiny shield, he snuck up on the terrifying Gorgon. By looking at her reflection in his shield, he was able to take careful aim and cut off her head—without turning to stone.

When King Polydectes refused to release Danae after Perseus presented him with Medusa's head, Perseus turned the trophy to stare at the king. Polydectes promptly turned to stone.[7] Perseus released his mother and they both escaped the island. Perseus gave the cap, sword, and sandals to Hermes. He gave Medusa's head to Athena, who mounted it on her shield.

Sisyphus, by the sixteenth-century Italian artist Tiziano Vecellio (also referred to as Titian), shows the eternal punishment Sisyphus received in the Underworld. Before his infamous flight from Hades, he was tricked by Autolycus, a son of Hermes.

HERMES

CHAPTER 4

Hermes the Thief and Hero

Sometimes Hermes used his powers for dishonorable gain. After all, he was the god of thieves. When he taught others to steal, chaos erupted.

Hermes had many children, one of whom was Autolycus (aw-TIL-ih-kus). Autolycus owned a small herd of cattle. His neighbor, Sisyphus (SIH-sih-fus), was king of Corinth, one of the wealthiest and most powerful Greek cities. He had a lot of cattle. Wanting to balance the size of the herds, Hermes taught Autolycus how to steal.

"If you turn Sisyphus' bulls into cows and change their colors to match your cows, then you can take them from under Sisyphus' watchful gaze," Hermes told his son.

The next day, Autolycus changed some of Sisyphus' cattle from white to red, and his black cows to white bulls. He then placed the changed cows among his herd. He repeated this for several days.

Sisyphus noticed the size of his herd decreasing and Autolycus' increasing. "Autolycus must be a thief," Sisyphus told himself. He thought of a plan to discover Autolycus' treachery. He marked the hooves of his remaining cattle with the letters *SIS*.

The next day, when more of his cattle disappeared, Sisyphus sent soldiers to Autolycus' cattle yard with directions to check their feet. After lifting the hooves of all the cattle, they found five marked SIS.

"He is a thief!" Sisyphus cried, pointing at Autolycus. "He has taken my cows and changed their colors so that I could not recognize them. Arrest him!"

As the soldiers grabbed his arms to twist them behind his back, Autolycus said, "I never stole those cows. They are my cattle." He

turned to Sisyphus. "When did you have cows of this color? You must be mistaken."

For several minutes everyone—Autolycus, Sisyphus, and the soldiers—argued and shouted. In the midst of the confusion, Sisyphus slipped into Autolycus' house and convinced his daughter to run away with him. She agreed, and the two traveled through many hills and countries. Several months later, they became the parents of the great Greek adventurer Odysseus (oh-DIH-see-us), who grew up to become one of the cleverest of the Greeks.[1]

Hermes may have been a rascal, but he did redeem himself on occasion. Homer's *Odyssey* recounts several occasions when the messenger god helps Odysseus on his ten-year-journey home from the Trojan War.

Circe (SIR-see, or KEER-kee), the daughter of the Greek sun god Helios (HEE-lee-ohs), could transform people into animals. When Odysseus' men arrived at her house on the island of Aeaea (ee-EE-uh), Circe offered them wine to drink that was drugged. The men turned into pigs.

One man from Odysseus' scouting party, Eurylochus (yuh-RIH-luh-kus), saw the event and reported it to Odysseus. The famous warrior left the ship, intent on rescuing his men. On the way he met Hermes, who knew what had happened. "I can help you rescue your men," Hermes said. "If you drink this herb"—he dug a black root bearing a milk-white bloom out of the earth—"it will prevent you from turning into a beast when she tries to harm you."

The plan worked as Hermes said. When Circe tried to force her wicked magic on Odysseus, he remained unchanged. Circe was so impressed that she fell in love with him and turned his companions back into men.[2] Odysseus and his men stayed in her house for a year, then set sail for more adventures around the world.

Another incident when Hermes helped Odysseus occurred months later when the ships in Odysseus' fleet wrecked near the island of Malta. Odysseus, the only survivor, washed ashore on a

A painting from 1682 shows the Greek warrior Odysseus visiting with Calypso, a goddess who fell in love with him and held him captive. Zeus heard Odysseus' cries for help and sent Hermes to convince her to let Odysseus return home.

small, secluded island. The nymph Calypso (kuh-LIP-soh) took him to her cave-home, where she tended his wounds. She, too, fell in love with him. "I'll give you eternal youth if you stay with me forever," she told him. He agreed, but after several years, Odysseus

tired of the beautiful island and yearned to leave. Calypso refused to help him.

In the Greek language, the name *Calypso* means "she who conceals." That is exactly what Calypso did for seven years—she hid from Odysseus any means of his sailing away. Unable to escape, Odysseus spent his days on the island standing at the water's edge, calling for help.

From his throne Zeus heard Odysseus' cries. He sent Hermes down to earth to intervene.

Hermes entered Calypso's grotto and greeted her. Calypso was glad for the company. "Have a seat, my lord, and sip my wine." She handed Hermes a cup.

Hermes took a sip, then said, "I am here on a mission, Calypso. Zeus, king of the gods, has heard Odysseus' cries and commands that you release him. The youth longs to explore the world."

Calypso choked back a sob, but whispered, "I will obey." No one argued with Zeus. Hermes hurried to tell Odysseus of his new-found freedom.

Calypso prepared sacks of corn, dried meat, wine, and water for Odysseus' journey. She also helped him construct a raft from cedar wood. Standing on the shore, she waved good-bye to her love as he sailed away, knowing she would never see him again.[3]

There is a similar story of a Trojan War hero lingering too long in the city of a queen, and the messenger god is called to intervene. Jupiter (the Roman equivalent of Zeus) sent Mercury (Hermes) to Carthage on the northern coast of Africa. There the Trojan warrior Aeneas had fallen in love with Dido, the city's queen. Mercury must remind Aeneas of his destiny to found his own city (Rome). He commanded him on behalf of Zeus to resume his voyage.[4] While Calypso was sad when her lover Odysseus left her island, Dido could not bear her grief over the loss of Aeneas. She cursed his descendants, then climbed on a funeral pyre piled with his possessions, fell on his sword, and died.[5]

The Children of Hermes

Like a lot of the Greek gods, Hermes had many children. His son Eudorus commanded a troop of soldiers in the Trojan War. Two other sons followed their brother onto the battlefield. More notable were Pan, Daphnis, Hermaphroditus, Myrtilus, and Autylocus.

Pan was born to the nymph Penelope. Unfortunately, she could not tolerate the sight of his body because the lower half resembled that of a goat. When Penelope ran away in distress, Hermes took Pan to Olympus, where the gods cared for him. Pan was the god of flocks, mountainous wilds, and rustic music, and was worshiped by shepherds.

Hermes and Aphrodite had a son, whose name was Hermaphroditus. After a pool of water fell in love with him, the two were combined, and the son came to have both male and female parts.

Hermes' son Myrtilus was a charioteer for King Oenomaus of Elis. He schemed with Pelops to beat Oenomaus in a race. Oenomaus was killed, but before he died he cursed Myrtilus, wishing that he would die at the hands of Pelops. Pelops did murder him, bringing upon himself a curse from Myrtilus. Hermes helped carry out this curse on Pelops' descendants: Atreus, Thyestes, Agamemnon, and Menelaus. Part of their heartache is told in the story of Jason and the Argonauts. Hermes immortalized Myrtilus by making him the constellation Auriga.

Pan teaches Daphnis to play a shepherd's pipe

Hermes often accompanied Zeus, such as when he stood ready to aid Zeus when he gave birth to Dionysus from his thigh. This vase painting shows him wearing his typical winged boots and a petasos (travelers cap) and holding his shepherd's staff. The royal scepter he holds belongs to Zeus.

HERMES

CHAPTER 5

The Wayfarers

Hermes sometimes lied and stole and taught thievery to others, but he could also exhibit extraordinary insight to the human condition. Perhaps one of the most touching examples of his compassion was when he and Zeus left Olympus one day to travel on a fact-finding trip around the world. Zeus wanted to know about the mortals he ruled. Were they friendly? How did they treat strangers? Did they show hospitality?

The two gods pretended to be poor wayfarers as they traveled. No one outside of Mount Olympus knew who they were when they knocked at the doors of houses, asking for food and shelter. For a long time, their reception was discouraging. Each time the two gods knocked on a door, begging for shelter and food, they were turned away.

After several months, the duo, weary and ravenous, reached a small, thatched hut on the outskirts of a village far from Mount Olympus (some say it was near Mount Parnassus). Hermes knocked on the wooden door. When an old woman opened it, he smiled at her.

"Good evening, my lady," Hermes said. "My friend and I are traveling throughout your fair land and have become hungry during our journey. We wondered if you might have a bite or two of food to share with us."

An old man joined the old woman at the door. The two stared at Zeus and Hermes for several long moments. The gods fidgeted under the elder pair's intense scrutiny, though no one could guess the bedraggled wayfarers' identities by their wan appearance. Dust covered their faces, and their clothing looked faded and worn. Still, the gods lowered their faces, lest some of their royalty show through.

"Welcome!" The old man swung open the door to the cottage. His name was Philemon (FIH-luh-mun). "My wife here will have a tidy supper ready that will fill those empty bellies."

The old woman, who introduced herself as Baucis (BAW-kus), added a smile of welcome before bringing them a wooden bowl of water to wash their grimy hands. Then Baucis raked out the fire, heaped on dried leaves and bark from the meager woodpile, and prepared a hot dish of herbs and bacon. As she stirred the pot, savory aromas filled the small abode. Hermes' stomach growled.

The couple's humble cottage might have been less fine than the castles on Mount Olympus, but the smiles on their hosts' faces and the soft places where Zeus and Hermes sat before a roaring fire were warm and pleasing.

With practiced hands, Baucis trimmed the cabbage her husband brought in from the garden just outside the door. Philemon took down a piece of cured meat from those hanging from the ceiling, cut it into strips, and put it into the kettle with the cabbage.

Baucis set out earthenware dishes, then offered the travelers olives, berries, radishes, cheese, eggs, and the stewed bacon. She served the cabbage soup, hot from the hearth, in scuffed but clean bowls. Dessert was apples and grapes picked from the orchard, and honey from a honeycomb.

Philemon and Baucis listened intently as their guests talked about the weather and the hazards of travel. The elderly couple took little food for themselves, preferring, they said, to listen rather than eat. Their apparently small appetites did not go unnoticed by the guests, who relished each bite of the meal and washed it all down with wine.

The first hint Philemon and Baucis had that their guests were no ordinary mortals was when Baucis tried to refill the soup bowls. She thought her eyes were deceiving her when the bowls refilled themselves as if by magic. Philemon noticed the same thing with the wine pitcher—though he refilled the cups, the pitcher never emptied.

The couple looked at each other in confusion. Suddenly, cold horror seized them. They realized they were in the presence of gods. The frightened couple fell to their knees before Zeus and Hermes. Raising their clutched hands, they tried to speak. "M-my lords," Philemon stammered, "w-we beg your mercy and patience. Our s-simple minds did not recognize you and w-we ask for another chance to provide a meal worthy of gods."

"Although," Baucis added, "I fear we have nothing left to serve but our old goose."

Hermes and Zeus helped the elderly couple to their feet. "Fear not, dear ones," Zeus told them. "The quality of the food you served was superb. What is more important is the gracious attitude that

Philemon and Baucis Giving Hospitality to Jupiter and Mercury, by Jean Restout. When Philemon and Baucis realize that Hermes and Zeus are gods, they prepare to kill their only goose for the strangers' dinner.

came with it. You served us the best you had, forgoing your own meal so that we would have enough. That is the true sign of a friend and what we had hoped to find in this land."

Then Zeus introduced himself as the king of the gods and Hermes as the god of safety and travels. Despite the king's kind words and manner, Baucis and Philemon trembled with fear.

Zeus and Hermes led Baucis and Philemon up a steep hill. At the top, the four stopped.

"Yours was the only hospitality we have seen," Zeus said. "This land is not fit to dwell in. The wretched place must be destroyed quickly."

Looking over the area below, Baucis and Philemon saw that it had already flooded. Their village was gone, and as far as they could see, there was nothing but water.

German painter Gerhard Jan Palthe also created the scene of Zeus and Hermes revealing themselves as gods to Philemon and Baucis.

Baucis and Philemon wept. It hurt to see what was familiar suddenly taken away. But they forgot their tears when they looked at their cottage. It seemed different—bigger and shinier. The couple blinked their eyes. Great marble columns, not crude timbers, braced the sloping roof. The thatched grass had been transformed into glistening gold. The kitchen garden and barnyard had become a beautiful marbled patio.

Zeus turned to the couple. "You will each be rewarded for your kindness with a granted wish. What is your dearest desire?"

Baucis and Philemon discussed the matter for several minutes. Finally, white-haired Baucis answered, "We would like to be your servants in that beautiful temple."

"So be it," Zeus replied. He turned to Philemon. "What would you wish for, my good man?"

"Never do I want to look at my dear wife's grave," said Philemon, "nor does she want to look at mine."

"Done."

For many pleasant years the old couple tended the lovely temple in comfort and pride. Then, one day, as they strolled through the forest around their home, Philemon saw green leaves in his dear wife's hair. She saw little sprigs in his. Lines began to appear on their faces as the lines in bark. They understood the meaning and welcomed it.

"Good-bye, my dear, sweet wife," said Philemon.

"Good-bye, sweet husband," said Baucis.

As Zeus had promised, the two became sturdy graceful trees, she a lime and he a majestic oak. The trees were said to grow so close together that one could imagine their intertwined branches growing from a single trunk.[1]

The stories written about Hermes fluctuate between episodes of honor and those of thievery and deception. Hermes was like most of us—not all good and not all bad. He started out his life on a mischie-

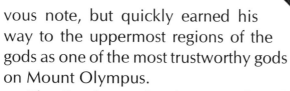

vous note, but quickly earned his way to the uppermost regions of the gods as one of the most trustworthy gods on Mount Olympus.

The Greek people who created myths about Hermes may have wanted to encourage listeners to think positively about life and themselves. Hermes showed us that we all can improve if we set our minds to it.

Biblical Story of the Flood

The Greek myth of Baucis and Philemon parallels a biblical story of the earth's destruction. The sixth chapter of the book of Genesis (JEH-nuh-sis) in the Bible relates the story of a great flood. After God created the world and mankind, he was displeased

Animals boarding Noah's ark

with mankind's behavior and decided to destroy the earth with water and start again. Just as God ruled over the earth, Zeus and Hermes held the destiny of their world in their hands. The gods chose to save Baucis and Philemon, just as the bibilical God chose to save Noah's family.

However, the two stories are not completely alike. The biblical account says God ordered Noah to build an ark on which Noah's family would live, along with two of every animal, until the rains subsided. He commanded that the rain fall for forty days and nights. Noah, his family, and all the species of animals floated safely in the ark, "high above the earth." Afterward, they lived on the earth together.

Baucis and Philemon saw their world destroyed when Zeus covered it with water. As a reward for their loyalty and kind hospitality, Baucis and Philemon lived the rest of their days in a temple built by Zeus. The Greek account says nothing about animals or other people. Nor does it give the ages of Baucis and Philemon when they died, though it does paint them as elderly.

God cared for Noah's family on the ark. Similarly, the lives of Baucis and Philemon ended with them melded together into a tree, their last wish granted by Zeus. Noah, who was mortal, died a natural death—at the great age of 950 years.[2]

Chapter 1. A Miraculous Birth

1. Malcolm Day, 100 *Characters from Classical Mythology* (Hauppauge, NY: Barron's Educational Series, 2007), p. 42.

2. Robert Graves, *The Greek Myths, Vol. I.* (New York: Penguin Books, 1977), p. 63.

3. *Homeric Hymn to Hermes*, trans. by H. G. Evelyn-White, lines 235–242, http://www.theoi.com/Text/HomericHymns2.html#4

4. Graves, p. 64.

5. Ron Leadbetter, "Hermes," *Encyclopedia Mythica* from *Encyclopedia Mythica Online*. http://www.pantheon.org/articles/h/hermes.html

6. Edith Hamilton, *Mythology* (Boston: Little, Brown and Company, 1969), p. 35.

7. Day, p. 42.

Chapter 2. Hermes Learns a Lesson

1. Robert Graves, *The Greek Myths, Vol. I* (New York: Penguin Books, 1977), p. 65.

2. Ron Leadbetter, "Hermes." *Encyclopedia Mythica* from *Encyclopedia Mythica Online*, http://www.pantheon.org/articles/h/hermes.html

3. Robert Graves, *Greek Gods and Heroes* (New York: Dell Publishing, 1960), p. 32.

4. Homer, *Odyssey*, trans. by Robert Fagles (New York: Penguin Putnam, 1996), Book 24, lines 1–5.

5. Ancient Scripts: Greek, http://www.ancientscripts.com/greek.html

6. Graves, *The Greek Myths*, p. 32.

7. Ibid., p. 184.

8. Ibid., p. 32.

Chapter 3. Hermes the Spy and Guide

1. Ron Leadbetter, "Hermes." *Encyclopedia Mythica* from *Encyclopedia Mythica Online*, http://www.pantheon.org/articles/h/hermes.html

2. Jenny March, *Cassell's Dictionary of Classical Mythology*, (London: Cassell & Co., 2001), p. 390.

3. Homer, *Odyssey*, trans. by Robert Fagles (New York: Penguin Putnam, 1996), Book 24.

4. Judgment of Paris, http://www.theoi.com/Olympios/JudgementParis.html.

5. Homer, *Iliad*, trans. by Robert Fagles (New York: Penguin Putnam, 1990), Book 24.

6. Robert Graves, *Greek Gods and Heroes* (New York: Dell Publishing, 1960), p. 25.

7. Apollodorus, *The Library*, translated by Sir James George Frazer (Loeb Classical Library, Volumes 121 & 122, Cambridge, MA: Harvard University Press, 1921), Book 2, http://www.theoi.com/Text/Apollodorus2.html#4

Chapter 4. Hermes the Thief and Hero

1. The Master Thief, http://www.timelessmyths.com/classical/heroes1.html#Thief.

2. Homer, *Odyssey*, trans. by Robert Fagles (New York: Penguin Putnam, 1996), Book 10, lines 388–399.

3. Ibid., Book 5, lines 1–265.

4. Vergil, *Aeneid*, trans. by Patric Dickinson (New York: New American Library, 1961), Book 4, line 278.

5. Ibid, lines 663–665.

Chapter 5. The Wayfarers

1. Edith Hamilton, *Mythology* (Boston: Little, Brown and Company, 1969), pp. 150–153.

2. *Holy Bible*, Genesis, Books 6–9.

FURTHER READING

For Young Adults

Barchers, Suzanne I. *From Atalanta to Zeus: Readers Theatre from Greek Mythology*. Santa Barbara: Libraries Unlimited, 2001.

Bulfinch, Thomas. *The Classic Treasury of Bulfinch's Mythology*. Philadelphia: Running Press Kids, 2003.

Greenblatt, Miriam. *Augustus and Imperial Rome*. Tarrytown, NY: Benchmark Books, 2000.

Hamby Zachary. *Mythology for Teens: Classic Myths for Today's World*. Austin, TX: Prufrock Press, 2009.

Kirk, Shoshanna. *Greek Myths: Tales of Passion, Heroism, and Betrayal*. San Francisco: Chronicle Books, 2005.

Nardo, Don. *Greek and Roman Mythology*. San Diego: Greenhaven Press, 2002.

Verniero, Joan. *An Illustrated Treasury of Read-Aloud Myths and Legends*. New York: Black Dog & Leventhal Publishers, 2004.

Works Consulted

Ancient Scripts: Greek, http://www.ancientscripts.com/greek.html

Apollodorus. *The Library*. Translated by Sir James George Frazer. Loeb Classical Library, Volumes 121 & 122. Cambridge, MA: Harvard University Press, 1921. Online at http://www.theoi.com/Text/Apollodorus2.html#4

Day, Malcolm. *100 Characters from Classical Mythology*. Hauppauge, NY: Barron's Educational Series, 2007.

Graves, Robert. *Greek Gods and Heroes*. New York: Dell Publishing, 1960.

Graves, Robert. *The Greek Myths, Vol. I*. New York: Penguin Books, 1977.

Hamilton, Edith. *Mythology*. Boston: Little, Brown and Company, 1969.

Homer. *Iliad*. Translated by Robert Fagles. New York: Penguin Putnam, 1990.

Homer. *Odyssey*. Translated by Robert Fagles. New York: Penguin Putnam, 1996.

Homeric Hymn to Hermes, trans. by H.G. Evelyn-White, http://www.theoi.com/Text/HomericHymns2.html#4

March, Jenny. *Cassell's Dictionary of Classical Mythology*. London: Cassell & Co., 2001.

Richardson, Donald. *Great Zeus and All His Children*. Englewood Cliffs, NJ: Prentice-Hall, Inc., 1984.

Vergil. *Aeneid*. Translated by Patric Dickinson. New York: New American Library, 1961.

On the Internet

Classical Mythology, Trojan War
http://www.timelessmyths.com/classical/greektrojan.html

Classical Myths: Hermes: Texts http://web.uvic.ca/grs/department_files/classical_myth/gods/hermes_t.html

Encyclopedia Mythica: "Hermes"
http://www.pantheon.org/articles/h/hermes.html.

Golden Age of Heroes: Autylocus, Master Thief
http://www.timelessmyths.com/classical/heroes1.html#Thief.

Hermes and the Golden Fleece
http://mythagora.com/bios/hermes.html#fleece.

Theoi Project: Hermes Family
http://www.theoi.com/Olympios/Hermes.html

ark—A large boat, such as the one built by Noah at God's command to save him and his family from the flood.

attaché (ah-tah-SHAY)—A messenger or spokesperson for an important official.

grotto (GRAH-toh)—A cave or cavern.

gynamsium (jim-NAY-zee-um)—A public sports place for the Greeks, who placed a high priority on physical strength.

herald (HAYR-uld)—Someone who brings or makes an announcement.

hieroglyphs (HY-roh-glifs)—Writing made up of drawn pictures.

hospitality (hos-pih-TAL-ih-tee)—The kind treatment of others, especially of guests or strangers.

league (LEEG)—A unit of distance, usually thought to be around three miles.

lyre (LYR)—A stringed musical instrument of ancient Greece; used to accompany singing and storytelling.

Maenad (MAY-nad)—A type of nymph known for fits of rage.

nymph (NIMF)—A maiden living in the sea, woods, or mountains who may assist a goddess.

pomegranate (PAH-muh-grah-nit)—Fruit with a red rind, filled with juicy red seeds.

pyre (PYR)—A large pile that, when lit during a funeral, a dead body is placed upon and burned as part of a funeral rite.

reception (ree-SEP-shun)—The response or reaction of one person as they meet another.

sinew (SIN-yoo)—A tendon.

wayfarer (WAY-fayr-er)—A traveler, especially one who is on foot.

INDEX